Geology Rocks!

Metamorphic Rock

Rebecca Faulkner

Raintree

Chicago, Illinois

© 2008 Raintree
a division of Reed Elsevier Inc.
100 N. LaSalle, Suite 1200, Chicago, IL 60602

Customer Service   888–363–4266
Visit our website at www.raintreelibrary.com

Editorial: Kathryn Walker, Melanie Waldron, and
Rachel Howells
Design: Victoria Bevan, Rob Norridge,
and AMR Design Ltd (www.amrdesign.com)
Illustrations: David Woodroffe
Picture Research: Melissa Allison and Mica Brancic
Production: Duncan Gilbert
Originated by Chroma Graphics Pte. Ltd
Printed and bound in China by
South China Printing Company

12 11 10 09 08
10 9 8 7 6 5 4 3 2 1

**Library of Congress Cataloging-in-Publication
Data**
Faulkner, Rebecca.
  Metamorphic Rock / Rebecca Faulkner.
    p. cm. -- (Geology Rocks)
  Includes bibliographical references and index.
  ISBN-13: 978-1-4109-2773-6 (lib. bdg.)
  ISBN-10: 1-4109-2773-3 (lib. bdg.)
  ISBN-13: 978-1-4109-2781-1 (pbk.)
  ISBN-10: 1-4109-2781-4 (pbk.)
  1. Metamorphic Rock--Juvenile literature. I. Title.
QE475.A2F39 2008
552'.4--dc22
                              2006037063

This leveled text is a version of *Freestyle:
Geology Rocks: Metamorphic Rock*.

Acknowledgments
The publishers would like to thank the following for
permission to reproduce photographs:

©Alamy p. **38** (Beateworks Inc.), p. **39 inset**
(Hugh Threlfall), p. 29 (Tom Till); ©Corbis p. **11**,
p. **4** (Galen Rowell), p. **39** (PhotoCuisine/Czap),
p. **36** (Reuters/Pascal Lauener); p. **32 left** (Ric
Ergenbright), p. **34** (Richard Hamilton Smith),
p. **42** (Robert Harding/Tony Waltham), p. **43**
(Tom Bean), p. **37** (Walter Hodges); ©GeoScience
Features Picture Library pp. **9, 13, 13 inset, 15, 21
top, 21 bottom, 33 right**, pp. **5, 33 left**
(D. Bayliss), p. **30** (Martin Land), pp. **5 middle
inset, 7, 10, 24 top, 24 bottom, 25, 26, 27, 28,
31, 35, 41, 44** (Prof. B. Booth); ©Getty Images
p. **12** (The Image Bank/John Lawrence); ©Harcourt
Education Ltd. p. **32 right** (Tudor Photography);
©NHPA p. **22** (Anthony Bannister), pp. **5 top inset,
23** (Bill Coster); ©Science Photo Library p. **20** (Daniel
Sambraus), p. **17** (Mauro Fermariello, p. **18** (NASA),
pp. **5 bottom inset, 40** (Photo Researchers)

Cover photograph of patterns on slate, Wales
reproduced with permission of ©FLPA
(Maurice Nimmo).

Every effort has been made to contact copyright
holders of any material reproduced in this book.
Any omissions will be rectified in subsequent
printings if notice is given to the publishers.

Disclaimer
All the Internet addresses (URLs) given in this book
were valid at the time of going to press. However,
due to the dynamic nature of the Internet, some
addresses may have changed, or sites may have
changed or ceased to exist since publication. While
the author and publishers regret any inconvenience
this may cause readers, no responsibility for any
such changes can be accepted by either the author
or the publishers.

CONTENTS

Some words are printed in bold, **like this**. You can find out what they mean by looking in the glossary. You can also look for them in the **On The Rocks!** section at the bottom of each page.

Squeeze and Heat

Rocks seem solid and steady. But over millions of years, rocks change. They can also be created and broken up.

Metamorphic rocks are rocks that have changed form. This usually happens deep inside Earth. It happens when rocks are heated and pressed.

The heated rocks become soft. They are squashed and folded. Then they become metamorphic rocks.

⇨ This is Mount Everest. It is the highest mountain on Earth. Mount Everest is mostly made of metamorphic rock.

Over time the rocks on the surface are worn away. Then the metamorphic rocks appear at the surface of Earth.

Most metamorphic rocks take millions of years to form. But there are situations where they can be created in an instant.

For example, this can happen when lightning strikes sand. The heat of the lightning melts the sand grains together. Metamorphic rock is formed.

⇩ **These metamorphic rocks have been bent and folded. You can clearly see folds in the rock.**

Find out later...

...how this **crater** was formed.

...what made these mountains.

...what type of metamorphic rock was used to make this building.

CRUST, MANTLE, AND CORE

Metamorphic rock is created by high temperatures and **pressures**. Pressure is weight or force pressing against something. There are high temperatures and pressures deep inside Earth.

Earth's layers

Earth is made up of layers. The **crust** is like the skin. It is the thinnest layer. There are two types of crust. They are continental crust and oceanic crust.

Continental crust lies beneath the land. It is up to 43 miles (70 kilometers) thick. Oceanic crust

Mountain crust
The crust is thickest under mountain ranges. Many metamorphic rocks make up this thickened crust.

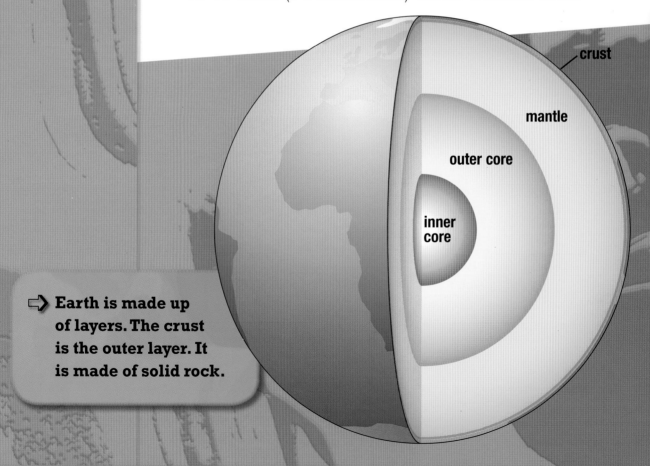

crust

mantle

outer core

inner core

⇨ Earth is made up of layers. The crust is the outer layer. It is made of solid rock.

   crust thin surface layer of Earth. It is made of rock.

is beneath the oceans. It is up to 6 miles (10 kilometers) thick.

Under the crust is the **mantle**. This layer is 1,800 miles (2,900 kilometers) deep. Temperatures here are up to 8,600° Fahrenheit (3,000° Celsius).

The **core** is at the center of Earth. There is a solid inner core and a liquid outer core. The inner core is made of hard metal. The outer core is melted metal.

Hot rocks!
The heat in the upper mantle and lower crust changes rock. It becomes metamorphic rock.

⬆ **This is an area in the country of Switzerland. Here we can clearly see Earth's rocky crust.**

Does the crust move?

Earth's **crust** is not one solid layer. It is broken up into huge moving pieces. These are called **plates**. They fit together like a giant jigsaw puzzle.

The plates float on the layer of Earth called the **mantle** (see page 6). They move very slowly over Earth. They move only a few inches each year. The plates carry the land and oceans with them.

In some places the plates are moving toward each other. When they meet, the crust may become

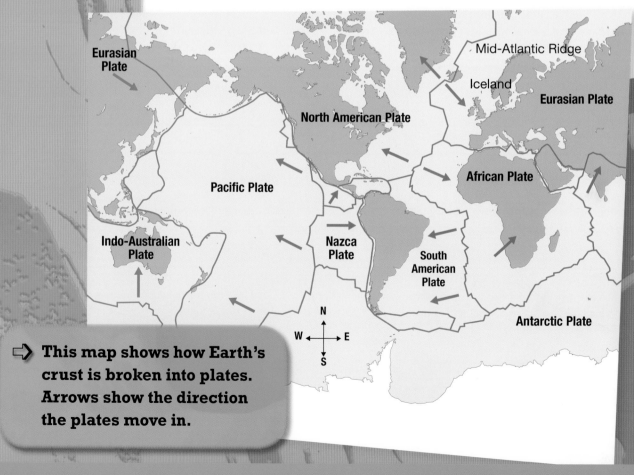

⇨ **This map shows how Earth's crust is broken into plates. Arrows show the direction the plates move in.**

squashed. It may be pushed down into Earth's mantle. Huge mountains or volcanoes can form.

In other places the plates are moving apart. This makes the crust weaker. It usually happens along mountain chains on the ocean floor. Hot melted rock rises at these places. It forces its way into the crust through cracks. It forms new rock.

fault

THE WORLD'S ROCKS

The whole of Earth's **crust** (top layer) is made of rocks. Rocks are in mountains and on the sea floor. They are in deserts and under ice. If you dig deep enough, you will always find rock.

What are rocks made of?

All rocks are made up of **minerals**. Minerals are found in nature. There are more than 4,000 types of minerals on Earth. Only about 100 of these are common in rocks.

⬇ **Some rocks create amazing landforms. These metamorphic rocks are in the Rocky Mountains in the United States.**

mineral   substance found in nature. Rocks are made from lots of minerals.

A rock may contain many different minerals. **Slate** is a metamorphic rock. It contains four minerals. They are quartz, feldspar, mica, and chlorite.

Quartzite is another metamorphic rock. It contains lots of quartz. Quartz is a hard mineral. This makes quartzite a hard rock.

Gneiss
The oldest rocks on Earth are about 4 billion years old. They are made of a metamorphic rock called **gneiss**. These rocks are found in the country of Canada.

⇧ **You can see the different minerals in this metamorphic rock.**

slate   metamorphic rock formed when the rock shale is flattened into sheets. This happens because of great pressure.

Earth's **crust** (top layer) is made of three groups of rock:

- igneous rock
- **sedimentary rock**
- metamorphic rock.

These rocks form in different ways.

Igneous rocks

Igneous rocks are made from **magma**. This is hot liquid rock. It forms in Earth's **mantle** (see page 6). Magma rises through the crust. As it rises it cools and hardens. It forms igneous rock.

⇦ **This is Giant's Causeway. It is in Northern Ireland in the United Kingdom. It is made of columns of basalt. Basalt is an igneous rock.**

Sedimentary rocks

Sedimentary rocks are formed from pieces of other rocks. Rain or wind breaks off these tiny pieces of rock. Wind or rivers carry them to a new place. The pieces pile up to form sedimentary rock.

Metamorphic rocks

Metamorphic rocks are rocks that have changed. Rising magma heats up the surrounding rocks. Movements in Earth's crust squash and fold the rocks over millions of years. This also makes the rocks soft. They change into metamorphic rocks.

Rock of sand
Sandstone is a sedimentary rock. It forms in areas where sand collects. The rock below is made of sandstone. It has been worn away into an arch.

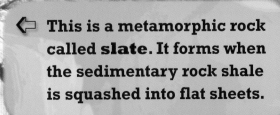

⇦ **This is a metamorphic rock called slate.** It forms when the sedimentary rock shale is squashed into flat sheets.

The rock cycle

Rocks are formed, broken down, and formed
again. This happens all the time. It is known as
the **rock cycle**.

Rocks are attacked by wind and rain as soon
as they appear on Earth's surface. This is called
weathering. Over millions of years, pieces of rock
are chipped off.

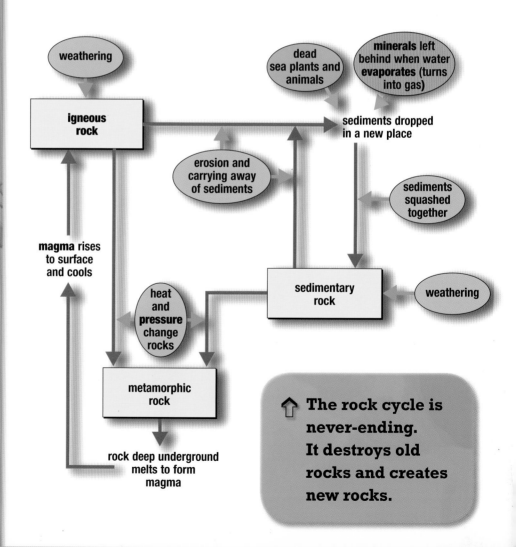

The rock cycle is
never-ending.
It destroys old
rocks and creates
new rocks.

Small pieces of rock are carried away by wind, rivers, or ice. When rock is worn and carried away, it is called **erosion**. The pieces are then dropped in another place. This is called **deposition**.

Over millions of years, the small pieces of rock pile up. These piles are known as **sediment**. Sediment changes into **sedimentary rock**. Then the rock cycle begins again.

In some areas Earth's **plates** (see page 8) crash into each other. The rocks there will be heated and squeezed. They change into metamorphic rock.

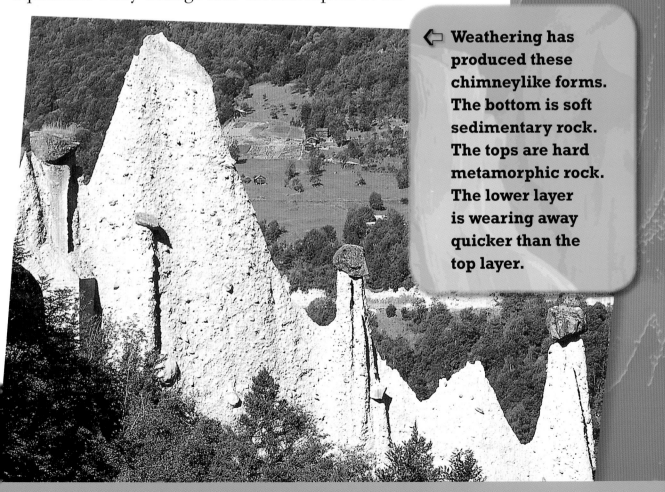

← **Weathering has produced these chimneylike forms. The bottom is soft sedimentary rock. The tops are hard metamorphic rock. The lower layer is wearing away quicker than the top layer.**

MARVELOUS METAMORPHISM

Magma
Magma has
a temperature
of about
2,000° Fahrenheit
(1,000° Celsius).
This is five times
hotter than a
very hot oven.

Metamorphic rocks form when existing rock is heated and pressed. This process of changing rocks is called **metamorphism**. It happens in different ways.

Contact metamorphism

Magma is hot melted rock. It rises from deep inside Earth. It pushes into other rocks as it rises. Magma heats up the rocks around it.

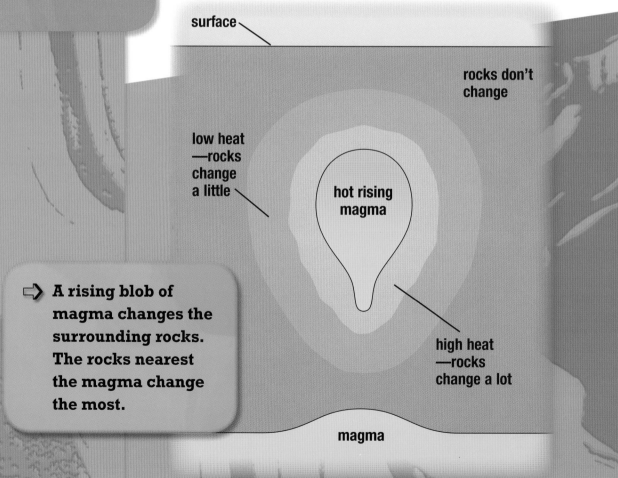

surface

rocks don't change

low heat —rocks change a little

hot rising magma

high heat —rocks change a lot

magma

⇨ **A rising blob of magma changes the surrounding rocks. The rocks nearest the magma change the most.**

Rocks are made up of materials called **minerals**. The scorching heat changes some minerals in the rock. They become new minerals. They form metamorphic rock.

This process is called **contact metamorphism**. It happens deep inside Earth's **crust** (top layer). Contact metamorphism also happens under volcanoes.

Marble
The white rock in this picture is **marble**. Marble is a metamorphic rock. It forms when the rock **limestone** is heated.

limestone   sedimentary rock made of calcite. Calcite is a mineral that makes up the shells of many sea creatures.

Regional metamorphism

Earth's **crust** (top layer) is made up of huge pieces of rock. These are called **plates** (see page 8). Earth's plates move slowly all the time.

Sometimes two plates crash into each other. The rocks may be squashed or pushed up. They may be buried under the growing mountains.

This action causes high **pressure**. Pressure is weight or force pressing down. It may also cause heating. The heat and pressure changes the rocks. They become metamorphic rocks.

⇩ **These are the Himalayas. They form the world's largest mountain range.**

plate giant, moving piece of Earth's crust

This process is called **regional metamorphism**. It changes rocks over a large area or region. Most metamorphic rocks form this way.

About 50 million years ago, the land that is now the country of India crashed into another plate. The rocks in between changed and piled up. They formed the mountain range called the Himalayas.

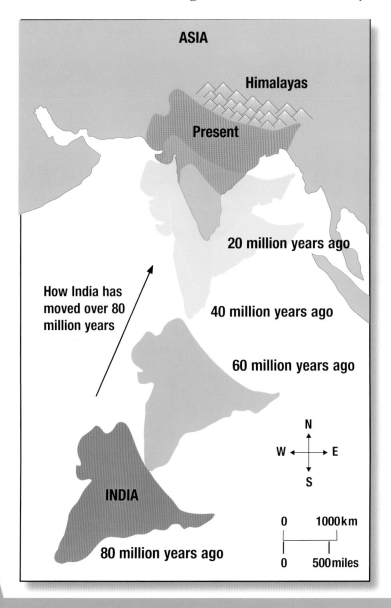

The Himalayan mountains were formed when India crashed into Asia.

Dynamic metamorphism

Rubbing and shaking

Rubbing and shaking

When two plates slide past each other, they rub together. This creates pressure in the crust. Sometimes this pressure causes an earthquake. Then the crust will move and shake.

In some places Earth's **plates** (see page 8) slide past each other. This can cause giant cracks in Earth's **crust** (top layer). These cracks are known as **faults**.

Rocks scraping past each other create **pressure**. Pressure is when weight or force presses against something. It causes rocks to change. They become metamorphic rocks.

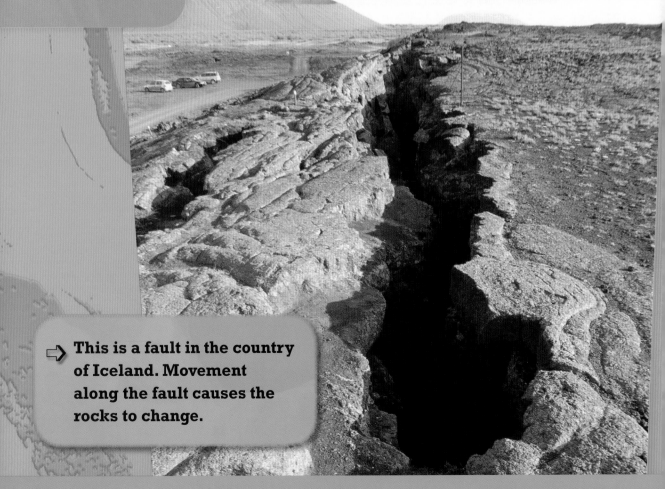

This is a fault in the country of Iceland. Movement along the fault causes the rocks to change.

This process is called **dynamic metamorphism**. It only happens in the narrow area around a fault.

The Moine Thrust is a fault zone. It is in the country of Scotland. Rocks along the fault slid past each other. This caused them to become soft and folded.

⇐ **This is the Moine Thrust in Scotland. You can see how the rocks have folded.**

⇒ **Rocks are made up of minerals. This rock is metamorphic rock. Its minerals have been squashed by heat and pressure.**

Impact metamorphism

Metamorphism is the process that changes rock. We have looked at three different types of metamorphism. They all happen over millions of years.

But there is one form of metamorphism that can happen instantly. This is called **impact metamorphism**. It happens very rarely.

⇩ This is the heaviest meteorite in the world. It crashed into Earth about 80,000 years ago.

meteorite   rock that has come from space and crash landed on Earth

A **meteorite** is a rock that has come from space. It crashes on Earth as a ball of fire. It is very unusual for this to happen.

When a meteorite hits Earth, it produces a **crater**. A crater is a dip that looks like a giant bowl. The force of the crash usually destroys the meteorite.

The great heat and force of the crash changes the surrounding rocks. They immediately become metamorphic rocks.

Large craters
Scientists have found more than 160 large meteorite craters around the world. Many more are hidden under the ocean.

⬆ A meteorite made this crater in the state of Arizona. The meteorite hit Earth about 50,000 years ago.

Melting rocks

Metamorphism mostly happens about 12 miles (20 kilometers) deep in the crust. The temperature there is about 1,800° Fahrenheit (800° Celsius).

What causes metamorphism?

Metamorphism is the process of forming metamorphic rocks. There are two main causes:

- increased heat
- increased **pressure** (weight or force pressing against something).

Heat

Rock is made up of solid materials called **minerals**. When rock is heated, its minerals may melt. This happens inside Earth's **crust**. It happens when **magma** (hot liquid rock) heats the surrounding

⬇ The rock on the left is **granite**. Pressure and heat turns it into the metamorphic rock **gneiss** (below).

granite a hard igneous rock

rocks. It may also happen when rocks are pushed deep into the crust (see page 9).

The rock cools when it gets closer to the surface. New minerals form. This creates metamorphic rock.

Pressure

The more rocks are pressing down, the more pressure there is. This happens deep in the crust. It happens under growing mountains. It also happens where the crust moves. Pressure changes the minerals in rock. They form metamorphic rock.

Hot water

Metamorphism can also be caused by water. Very hot water is found deep in the crust. It can change surrounding rocks by heating them.

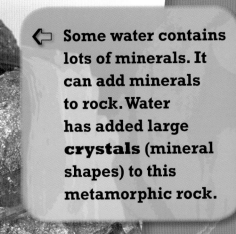

Some water contains lots of minerals. It can add minerals to rock. Water has added large **crystals** (mineral shapes) to this metamorphic rock.

Grouping metamorphic rock

The type of metamorphic rock formed will depend on two main things:

- the type of **parent rock**
- the **metamorphic grade**.

Parent rock

The parent rock is the type of rock that changed to make metamorphic rock.

Quartzite is a common metamorphic rock. Its parent rock is **sandstone**. Heat and **pressure** (weight pressing down) change sandstone into quartzite.

Parent rocks

Parent rock	Metamorphic rock
shale	slate
shale, slate, basalt, granite	schist
shale, slate, schist, granite	gneiss
limestone	marble
sandstone	quartzite

⬆ **This is the metamorphic rock slate. It forms from the rock shale. Pressure has flattened and lined up the minerals.**

　parent rock　type of rock that existed before metamorphism

Metamorphic grade

All metamorphic rocks are given a grade. This grade depends on how much heat and pressure changed the rock. Rocks may show low-, medium-, or high-grade **metamorphism**.

Great heat and pressure causes high-grade metamorphism. These rocks are greatly changed. Much lower heat and pressure causes low-grade metamorphism. The rocks change only a little.

⇩ **This is the metamorphic rock gneiss. Great heat and pressure are needed to form gneiss.**

We can group metamorphic rocks in two other ways:

- amount of **foliation** (banding or layering)
- grain size and **texture** (how something feels).

Foliation

Metamorphic rocks can be separated into **foliated** and **nonfoliated rocks**. In foliated rocks the **minerals** are squashed into bands. Nonfoliated rocks do not have bands.

Foliated rocks

Some foliated rocks have light and dark bands. These bands may also be folded. This creates wavy patterns in the rock.

These rocks are foliated (layered). They have been formed by great **pressure** (weight pressing against them).

bands

Grain size and texture

We can also group metamorphic rocks by the size of their grains and their texture. Grains are the mineral parts that make up rock. Texture is how the rock feels.

The texture is usually named after the metamorphic rock. For example, the rock **slate** has fine grains. It splits easily. We say it has a slaty texture. The rock **schist** has large grains. Its minerals are long and thin. This is a schistose texture.

Different sizes
The rock in this picture has some large grains among lots of small grains. We call this a porphyroblastic texture.

Metamorphic Rock Types

Minerals are the materials that make up rocks. In **foliated** rock the minerals are arranged in bands or layers. The following types of rock are all foliated.

Gneiss

Gneiss is a **coarse-grained** rock. This means it has large mineral parts. Gneiss is usually pink or gray.

Gneiss often has clear light and dark bands. These may be folded.

Fossils

Slate sometimes contains **fossils**. These are the remains of plants or animals. In slate the fossils are often squashed or folded.

⬆ This is the metamorphic rock slate. We can see a fossil in this rock.

fossil remains of a dead plant or animal found in a rock

Schist

There are many different types of **schist**. They are all foliated. The layers often look folded. Schist can be fine- medium-, or coarse-grained. The minerals in it are often long and thin.

Slate

Slate is a very **fine-grained** rock. The mineral grains are too small to see. Slate is usually black or gray. It sometimes has a slight blue or green color. Slate can be split easily into thin sheets.

⇩ **This mountain is formed from the metamorphic rock schist.**

The following types of metamorphic rocks are **nonfoliated** rocks. These rocks do not have bands.

Marble

The **minerals** that make up **marble** are a medium size. We say that marble is a **medium-grained** rock.

The **parent rock** of marble is **limestone**. This means that heating and squashing turns limestone into marble. Marble is usually white. But it may contain patches or streaks of gray, black, red, or green.

The parent rock for marble (left) is limestone (below). Heating and squashing changes limestone into marble.

Quartzite

Quartzite is another medium-grained rock. It forms when the rock **sandstone** is heated or squashed. Quartzite is white or gray in color.

Hornfels

Hornfels is made up of fine mineral grains. It forms when rocks such as mudstone are heated. Hornfels is usually gray or black. It may have a slight blue or green color.

⇩ Sandstone (below) is the parent rock of quartzite (left). Heat changes **sandstone** into quartzite.

How can we identify metamorphic rocks?

Every day you see rocks of all shapes and sizes. You see them in buildings and in nature.

But how do you tell if a rock is metamorphic or not? Look at the rock closely. **Minerals** are the materials that make up rock. Look carefully at them. Ask yourself some questions:

- Do the minerals all face the same direction?
- Do the minerals look squashed?

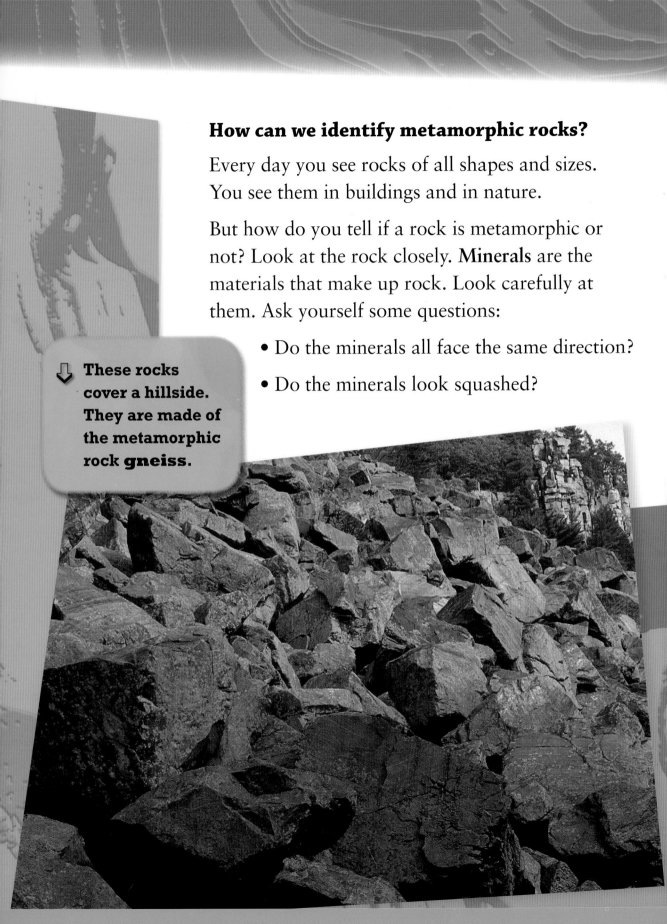

⇩ **These rocks cover a hillside. They are made of the metamorphic rock gneiss.**

- Are there bands or layers in the rock?

- Do the layers in the rock look twisted or folded?

Can you answer "yes" to any of these questions? If you can, then the rock may be metamorphic.

Scientists sometimes use **microscopes** to study tiny pieces of rock. A microscope makes things look bigger. It allows scientists to see what the rock contains. Then they can work out what kind of rock it is.

⇩ This is a piece of gneiss seen under a microscope. You can see the different minerals in the rock.

microscope   device used to see very small objects. It makes them appear bigger.

Hard Beauty

You know what metamorphic rocks look like. Now look out for the different ways people use them.

Building stones

Metamorphic rocks have been formed by scorching hot temperatures. They are also formed by huge weights pressing against them.

Heating and squashing makes metamorphic rocks very tough. Because of this, metamorphic rocks make good building materials.

➡ The floor of this fountain is made from gneiss. Gneiss is a hard stone. It lasts a long time.

marble   metamorphic rock formed when limestone is heated

Marble and gneiss are very tough rocks. They are often used as building stones. Marble is also very beautiful and easy to cut. It has been used in lots of amazing buildings.

Marble is used for statues and staircases. Many people use it for kitchen and bathroom surfaces. Marble is easy to clean and looks good.

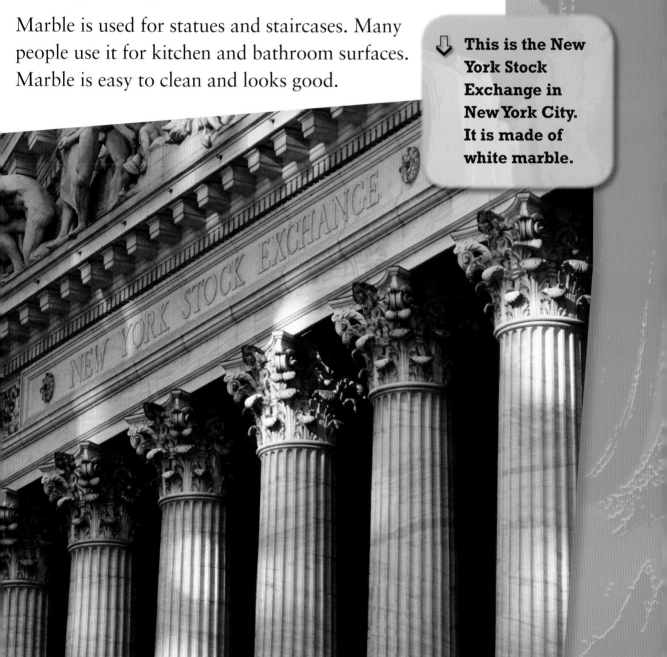

⇩ This is the New York Stock Exchange in New York City. It is made of white marble.

gneiss   metamorphic rock with large grains. It is formed under great pressure.

Roofs and floors

Slate is easily split into thin layers. It stands up well to **weathering**. Weathering is when the weather attacks rock. Slate is a perfect material for roof tiles. It is also great for floor tiles and paving stones.

⇩ Slate is often used to make floor tiles for kitchens and bathrooms.

Slate in schools

In the past slate was used by schoolchildren. Each child had a writing slate. They used chalk to write on it.

Minerals are the materials that make up rock. The metamorphic rock **schist** contains some very useful minerals. Talc is one of them. Talc is used to make paint, paper, and baby powder.

Quartzite is a very hard rock. It is used in road and railroad building.

⇩ This kitchen equipment is made from stainless steel. Stainless steel contains the mineral chromium. This comes from schist.

Valuable rocks
Schist can contain gold and garnet. Garnet is a mineral used in jewelry. The ring shown here is made with gold and a red garnet.

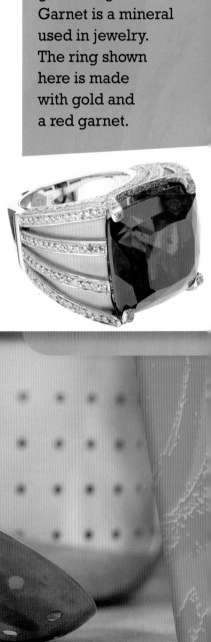

METAMORPHIC LANDFORMS

Metamorphic rocks mostly form underground. In some places they appear at Earth's surface. They appear when the soil and rocks above them are worn away.

Metamorphic rocks are very tough. They do not wear away easily.

Metamorphic mountains

Split Mountain is in the state of California. It has layers of metamorphic and **igneous rock** (see page 12).

A blob of **magma** (hot melted rock) formed the igneous rock. The magma rose into Earth's **crust** (top layer).

⬇ **This is the metamorphic rock gneiss. It formed deep underground. The rocks above it wore away.**

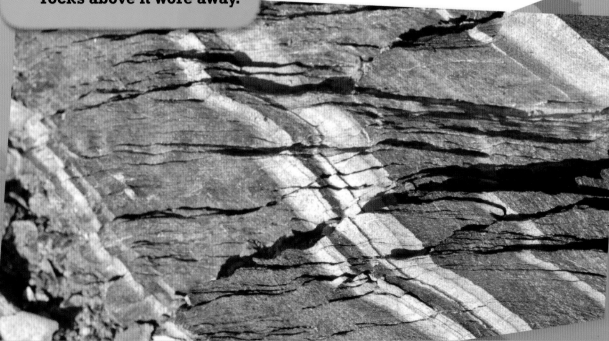

igneous rock rock formed from hot liquid rock (magma) either underground or at Earth's surface

It heated the surrounding rocks. This created the metamorphic rocks.

Huge mountain ranges form when two **plates** (see page 8) crash together. This causes a large area of rock to become metamorphic rock.

Over time the metamorphic rocks appear at the surface. They form part of all major mountain chains.

⇩ **This is the Alps mountain range in southern Europe. It formed where two plates crashed together.**

Folds and bands

Rocks are **metamorphosed** (changed) when mountains form. Rocks also metamorphose along **fault** lines. Faults are giant cracks in Earth's crust.

These metamorphic rocks are often folded. After millions of years, they appear at Earth's surface. These folds will still be there.

⬇ **This is the metamorphic rock gneiss. The light and dark bands show where the rock was folded.**

Whistler is a ski resort in the Rocky Mountains in the country of Canada. The mountains there are made of very old metamorphic rocks. These metamorphic rocks formed deep inside Earth.

Over millions of years, the mountains above them **eroded** (wore away). Now the metamorphic rocks have appeared at the surface.

Piles of rubble
The town of Whistler is built on the metamorphic rock **schist**. Schist breaks easily. This produces piles of rubble at the bottom of cliffs.

⇩ **This beautiful metamorphic rock is quartzite. It shows very clear bands (layers).**

Summary

- There are three main types of rock. Metamorphic rock is not as common as the other types.

- Most metamorphic rocks begin their life deep in Earth's **crust** (top layer). Existing rocks change into metamorphic rocks. Heat, **pressure** (weight pressing down), and hot water make this happen.

- Over millions of years, the rock above the metamorphic rocks is **eroded** (worn away). Then the metamorphic rocks appear at Earth's surface.

- Metamorphic rocks are tough and lasting. They often form mountains.

- There are many types of metamorphic rock. The type depends on the kind of rock they form. It also depends on the amount of heat and pressure that formed them.

- We use metamorphic rocks for buildings and statues. We also use them in jewelry.

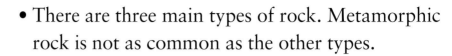

⇨ **A tube of magma** (hot liquid rock) has baked the rocks around it. This heating has formed metamorphic rock.

FIND OUT MORE

Books

Bingham, Caroline. *Rocks and Minerals*. New York: DK, 2004.

Harman, Rebecca. *Rock Cycles* (Earth's Processes). Chicago: Heinemann, 2005.

Pellant, Chris and Helen. *Marble and Other Metamorphic Rocks* (Guide to Rocks and Minerals). Milwaukee, WI: Gareth Stevens, 2007.

Stewart, Melissa. *Metamorphic Rocks* (Rocks and Minerals). Chicago, Heinemann, 2002.

Using the Internet

If you want to find out more about metamorphic rock you can search the Internet. Try using keywords such as these:

- meteorite
- gneiss
- marble.

You can also use different keywords. Try choosing some words from this book.

Try using a search directory, such as www.yahooligans.com

Search tips

There are billions of pages on the Internet. It can be difficult to find what you are looking for. These search skills will help you find useful websites more quickly:

- Know exactly what you want to find out about.
- Use two to six keywords in a search. Put the most important words first.
- Only use names of people, places, or things.

GLOSSARY

basalt type of igneous rock formed when lava cools and solidifies

coarse grained rock with large grains

contact metamorphism changes in rock caused by hot liquid rock (magma) rising through the crust. The magma heats and changes the surrounding rocks.

core center of Earth

crater circular dip

crystal structure within a mineral

crust thin surface layer of Earth. It is made of rock.

deposition laying down weathered rock in a new place

dynamic metamorphism changes in rock caused by plates (pieces of Earth's crust) rubbing together

erode wear away and remove

erosion wearing away and removal of weathered rock

fault giant crack in Earth's crust

fine grained rock with small grains

foliated rock that has bands or layers

foliation banding or layering

fossil remains of a dead plant or animal found in a rock

gneiss metamorphic rock with large grains. It is formed under great pressure.

granite a hard igneous rock

hornfels metamorphic rock formed during contact metamorphism

igneous rock rock formed from hot liquid rock (magma) either underground or at Earth's surface

impact metamorphism changes in rock caused by sudden heat or pressure. This can happen when a meteorite hits Earth or lightning strikes.

lava name for magma when it reaches Earth's surface

limestone sedimentary rock made of calcite. Calcite is a mineral that makes up the shells of many sea creatures.

magma hot melted rock from inside Earth

mantle hot layer of Earth beneath the crust

marble metamorphic rock formed when limestone is heated

medium grained rock with grains of medium size

metamorphic grade amount of metamorphism, or change

metamorphism process by which rocks change

metamorphose change

meteorite rock that has come from space and crash landed on Earth

microscope device used to see very small objects. It makes them appear bigger.

mineral substance found in nature. Rocks are made from lots of minerals.

non-foliated rock that does not have bands or layers

parent rock type of rock that existed before metamorphism

plate giant, moving piece of Earth's crust

pressure force or weight pressing against something

quartzite very hard metamorphic rock

regional metamorphism changes in rock across a large area. This is caused by heat and pressure, usually where mountains are forming.

rock cycle unending cycle of rock formation and destruction

sandstone sedimentary rock made from sand

schist metamorphic rock. It is formed by great pressure.

sediment pieces of rock that have been worn away and moved to another place

sedimentary rock rock formed from the broken pieces of other rocks

shale sedimentary rock made from mud

slate metamorphic rock formed when the rock shale is flattened into sheets. This happens because of great pressure.

texture how something feels

weathering breaking down of rock by the weather

INDEX